Book 1

Jazz Menagerie

7 Light-Hearted Solos in a Variety of Styles for the Late Elementary Pianist

Catherine Rollin

Animals are such a wonderful source of inspiration for the musical imagination! There is an endless variety of shapes, sizes, sounds and personalities in the animal kingdom. The pieces in *Jazz Menagerie* draw upon this vast and colorful resource. I hope this whimsical menagerie, with its hints of jazz sounds and rhythms, will delight, entertain and spark the imagination of late elementary pianists.

Catherine Rollin

Contents

Alfred

Cover art: David Gardner • Cover design: Ruth McKinney

Bear and Birdie Waltz

Catherine Rollin

Leisurely, and with humor

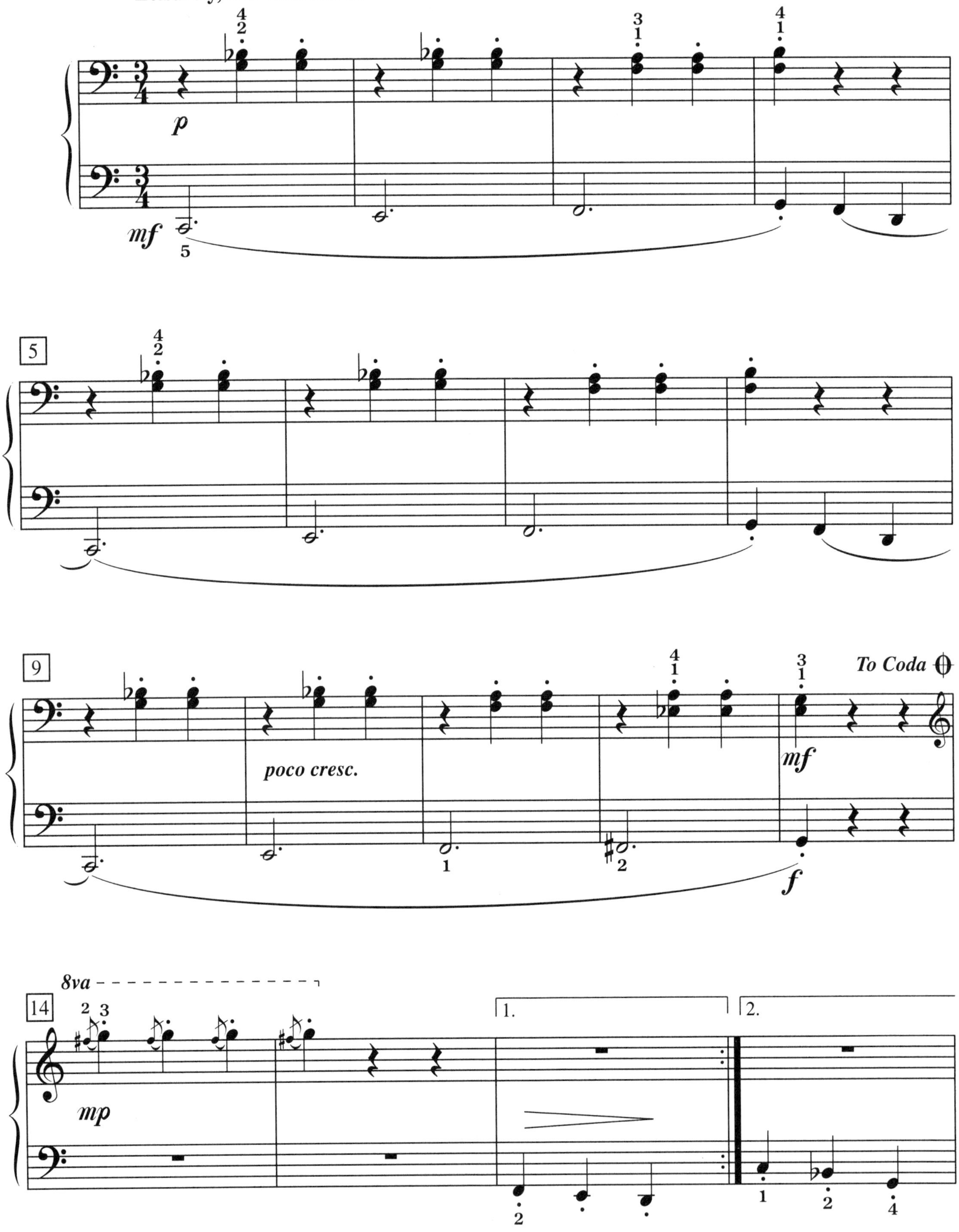

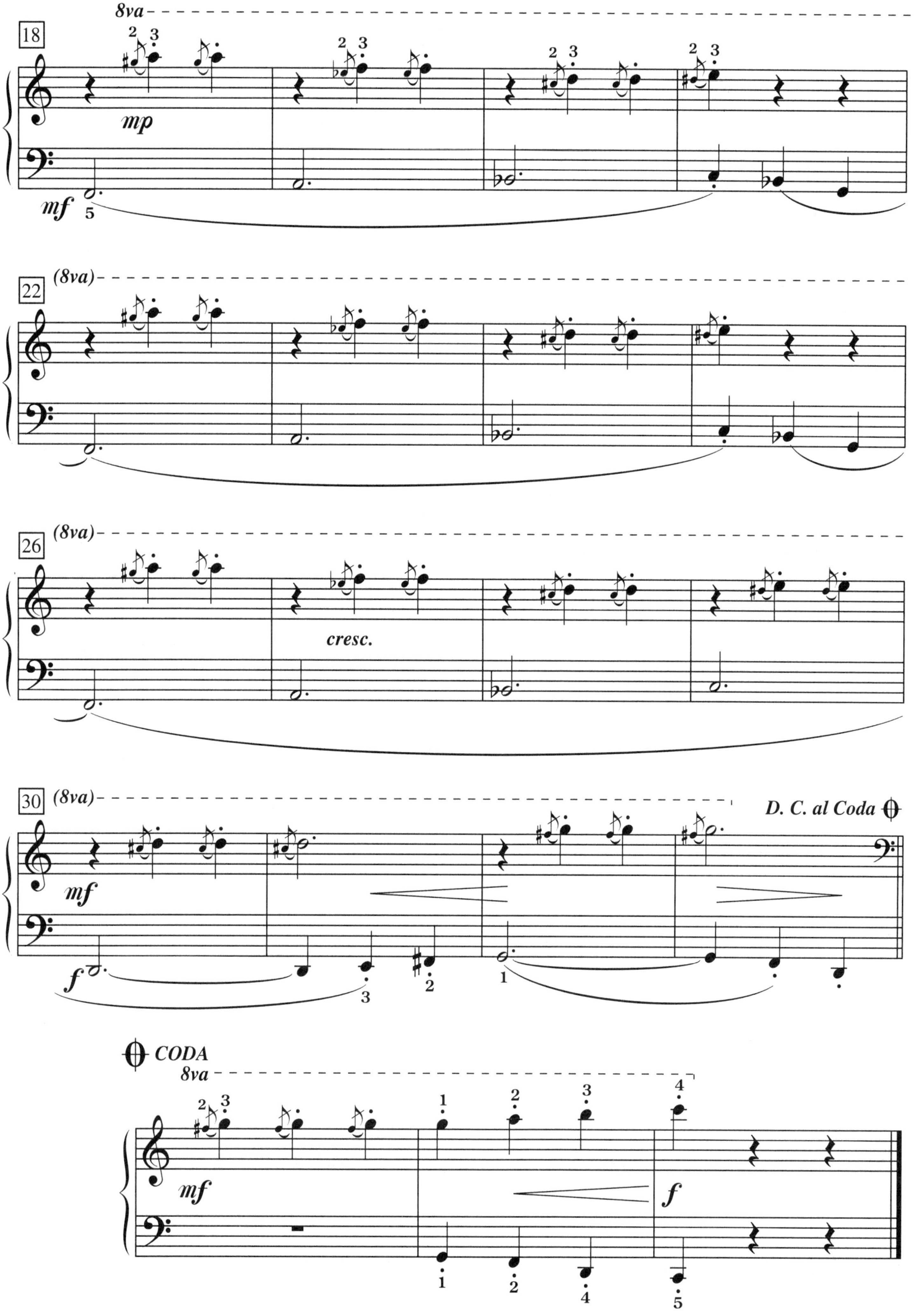
18
8va
mp
mf
22
(8va)
26
(8va)
cresc.
30
(8va)
D. C. al Coda
mf
f
CODA
8va
mf
f

Parrot Blues

Moderately and conversational

Catherine Rollin

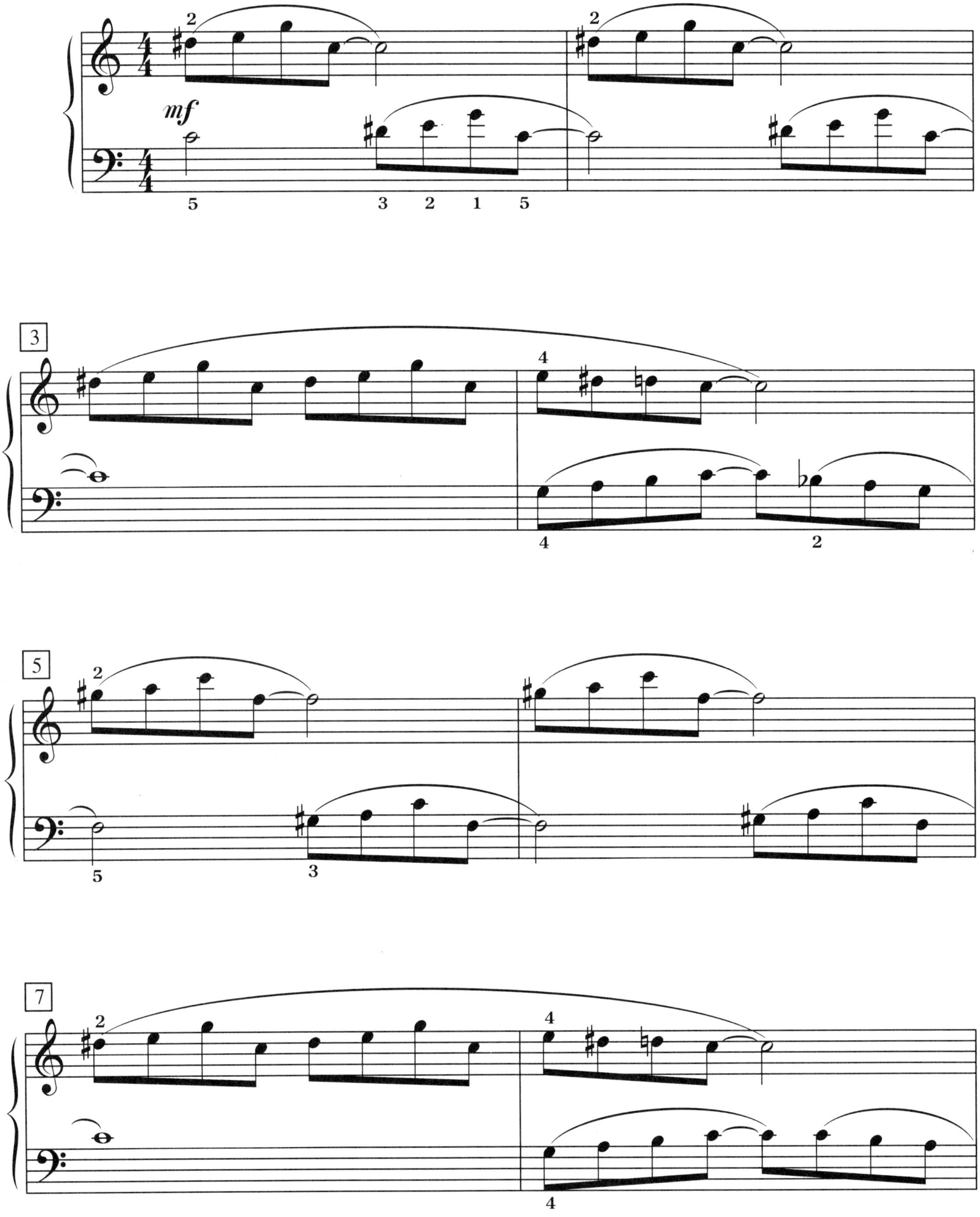

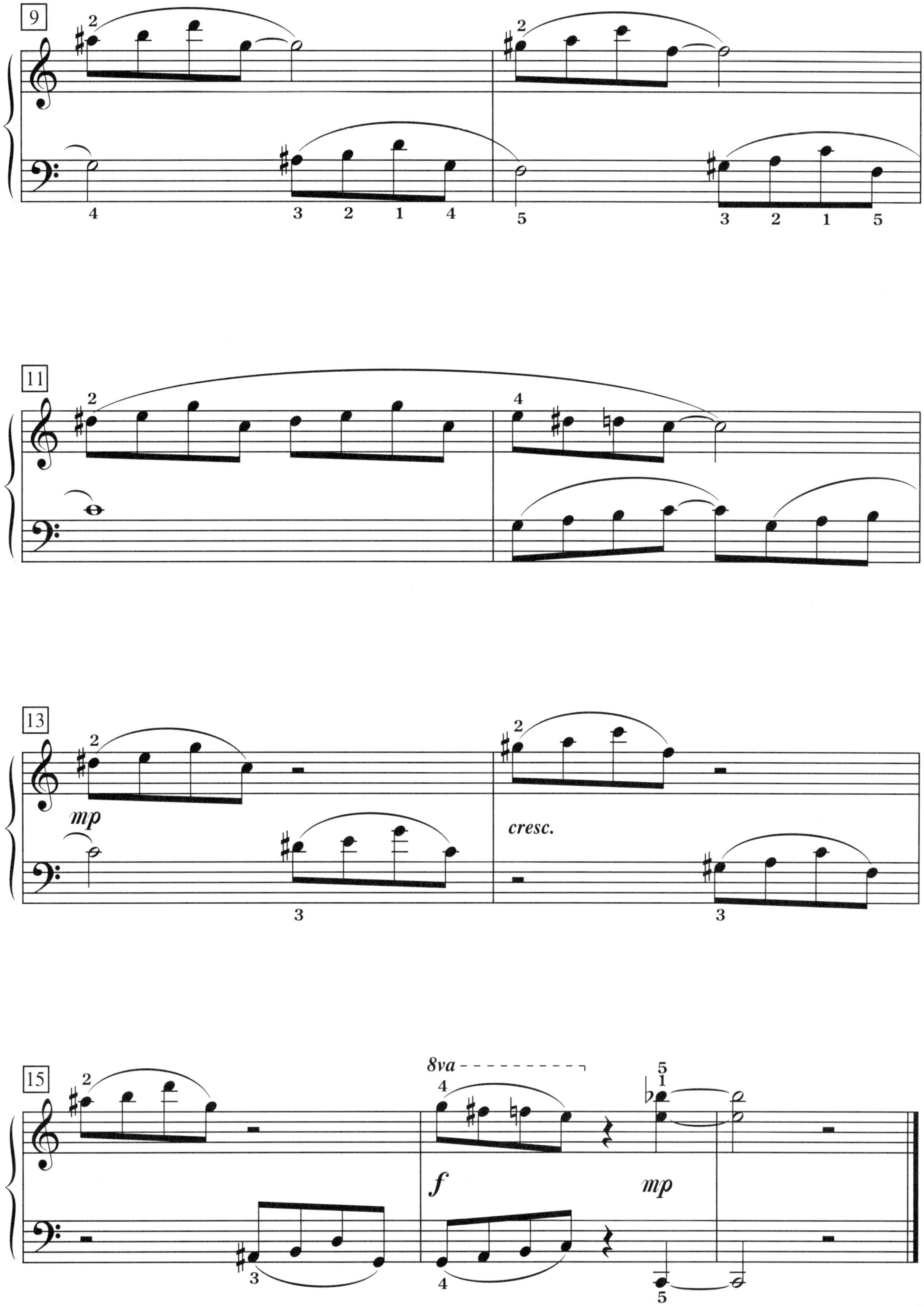
9
11
13
mp
cresc.
15
8va
f
mp

Penguin Waddle Rag

Catherine Rollin

Allegretto, with humor and cheer

17
mf
f
21
mp
25
mf
29
mf
f

Camel's Back Blues

Moving along

Catherine Rollin

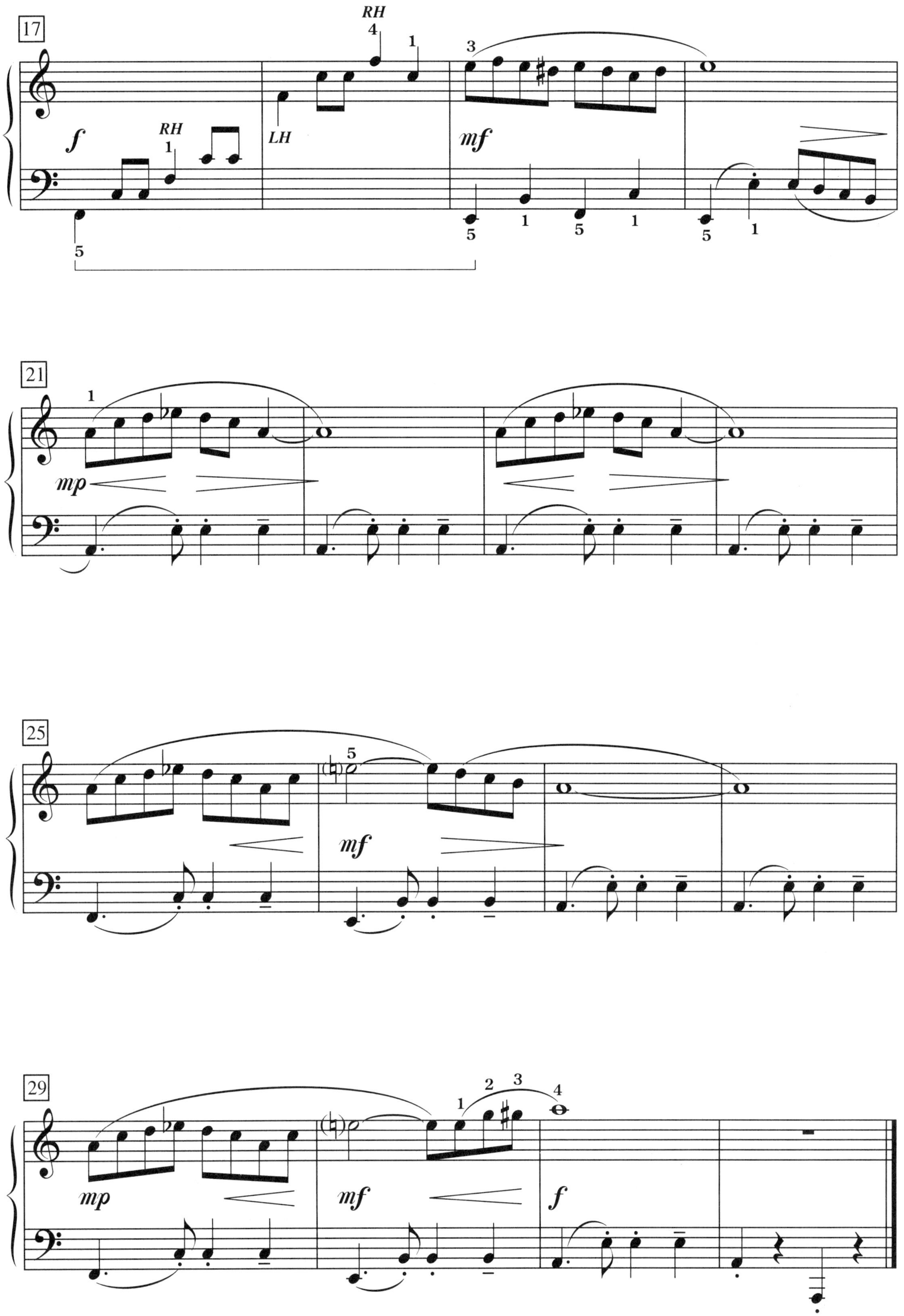
17
RH
LH
f
mf
21
mp
25
29

The Hip Hoppity Frog

Allegretto—happily and aim carefully so as not to fall in the water

Catherine Rollin

13
8va
RH
LH
p
cresc.
16
f
mp
19
p
22
RH
LH
p
26
8va
RH
LH
cresc.
8va
f

Tiger Boogie

Catherine Rollin

Fairly fast and mysteriously

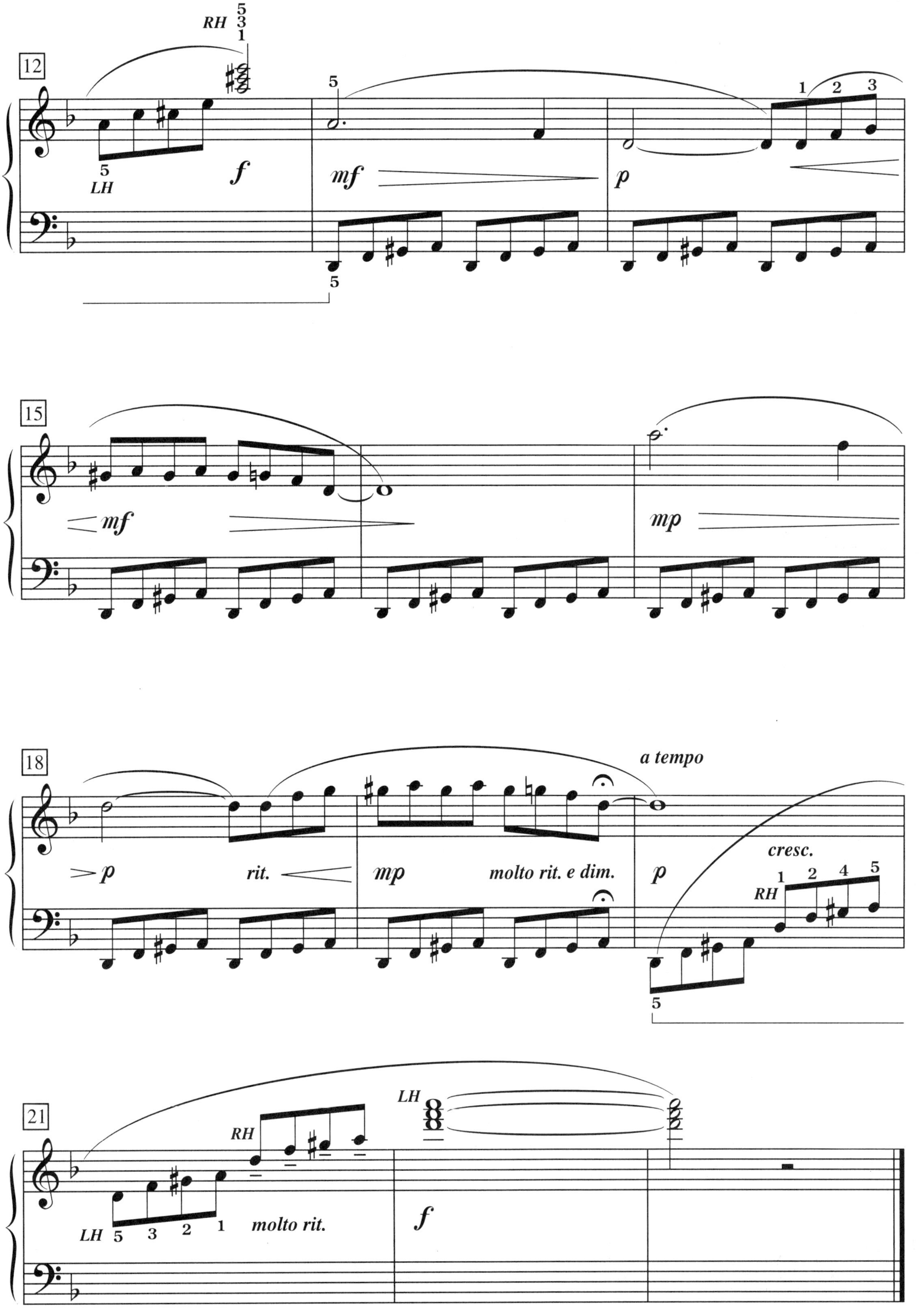
12
RH
LH
f
mf
p
15
mf
mp
18
a tempo
p
rit.
mp
molto rit. e dim.
p
cresc.
RH
21
LH
RH
LH
molto rit.
f

Woodpecker's Peckin' Party

Fairly quickly, with sharp peckin' staccatos

Catherine Rollin

* In the upper treble clef, (ms. 25-44), all stems down are played by the left hand, and should be slightly emphasized.

33
mf
37
mp
41
mf
45
cresc.
f
49
mp
cresc.
f